OVER THE HEDGE 3
Knights of the Picnic Table

Other Books

Over the Hedge 2
Over the Hedge

Also by Michael Fry

Send in the Stunt Mom
What I Want to Be When THEY Grow Up

Over the Hedge 3
Knights of the Picnic Table

Michael Fry and T Lewis

**Andrews McMeel
Publishing**

Kansas City

Over the Hedge is distributed internationally by United Feature Syndicate, Inc.

Over the Hedge 3: Knights of the Picnic Table copyright © 1997 by United Feature Syndicate, Inc. All rights reserved. Printed in the United States of America. No part of this book may be used or reproduced in any manner whatsoever without written permission except in the case of reprints in the context of reviews. For information, write Andrews McMeel Publishing, 4520 Main Street, Kansas City, Missouri 64111.

www.andrewsmcmeel.com

ISBN: 0-8362-3731-5

Library of Congress Catalog Card Number: 97-71632

Over the Hedge and **Committed** may be viewed on the Internet at:
www.unitedmedia.com

Send Michael Fry and T Lewis e-mail at:
Fry1@flash.net

To Sarah and Emily,
for laughing with me.
And at me.

—MF

To my big sisters, Pam and Leslie . . .
for resisting the urge
to drop me on my head as a baby.

—TL

Foreword

What can you say about Verne and RJ, or Mike Fry and T Lewis for that matter? For one, T and RJ share the handicap of no first name. Mike and Verne share an unfortunate lack of follow-through on their golf swings. What they all have in common are origins in that strange, semi-utopian, Twilight Zone world that exists on the cutting edge of civilization: close to nature, but not too far away from the 7-Eleven. That place just beyond those surreally marked exits on the interstate that declare with Zen koan-like clarity, "If you lived here you'd be home by now."

And we all do live there now, don't we? In that all-too-familiar world of small yards and big screens. That world of dual incomes and numbing architectural repetition. That fresh-scrubbed, tightly controlled world Steven Spielberg deified for us all. The American Suburb. Like good reporters, Mike and T have revealed to us at last what lies just beyond those well-groomed hedges and answered, once and for all, the mystery of disappearing remote controls. They haven't been swallowed by hungry sofa cushions or accidentally made their way into the trash. No. They have been pilfered by that band of TV-addicted, Frito-crunching forest creatures who take over our big screens and hot tubs at night. Those denizens of secret burrows, tunnels, and crawl spaces who love nothing more than a night of Lucy reruns and a bag of marshmallows. Those creatures who know who we are, and what we like, better than we do ourselves. Those creatures who live just *Over the Hedge.* . . .

—Jim Cox, screenwriter, producer, *Oliver & Co.*, *Ferngully*,
Beauty and the Beast, and the upcoming *Over the Hedge* movie

"...AND ANOTHER THING, SANTA... WITH FEDEX AND THE INTERNET BREATHIN' DOWN YOUR NECK, WHO HAS *TIME* FOR *CLIMBING* DOWN *CHIMNEYS*???

....HERE'S THE *TICKET:*...

BETTER WATCH OUT... BETTER NOT CRY...

.... *TRAINED FERRETS...* THEY'RE *IN*... THEY'RE *OUT*... NO *MUSS*...NO *FUSS*...

...BETTER NOT POUT... I'M TELLIN' YOU WHY...

FRYe LEWIS

...NO *CHIMNEY?* NO *PROBLEM!*... THEY'LL GO THROUGH A DRYER VENT LIKE *SALSA* THROUGH A *GOOSE!*

...SANTA WEASEL'S COMIN' TO TOWN!...

NO! NO! NO!... I WANT MY SANTA *PLUMP, JOLLY* AND BEARING *BOUGHS OF HOLLY!!*

MY RESEARCH SAYS THAT'S NOT A MARKETABLE...

GIVE ME BACK MY SANTA!!

FRYe LEWIS

BOOTS!... NO GUCCI'S!!

YOU'RE A CRUEL LITTLE TURTLE.

VERNE...YOU *WON'T* SURVIVE.

CAN'T YOU BE A *BIT* MORE POSITIVE?

OKAY...VERNE... YOU *WILL* DIE.

MAYBE NOT QUITE *SO* POSITIVE.

OKAY...

...VERNE...YOU MIGHT NOT DIE, BUT YOU'LL NEVER TAP YOUR TOES TO "BRANDY" AGAIN.

I CAN LIVE WITH THAT.

VERNE, SKIING OFF THIS WILL ONLY *CONFIRM* WHAT WE ALL *SUSPECT.*

RIGHT! THAT I'M A WILD-EYED TERRAPIN, CAPABLE OF INCREDIBLE FEATS OF DARING!!

NO... THAT YOU'RE

A *MORON?!!*

SO WHY PROVE IT AND REMOVE ALL DOUBT?

A *REAL PAL* WOULD SHOW ME HOW TO DO THIS, R.J.

VERNE...

...WHEN YOU SKI OFF INTO OBLIVION... *WHO'S* GOING TO CLEAN UP THE *MESS?...*

UH...

...AND ISN'T *THAT* WHAT REAL PALS ARE FOR?

UH...

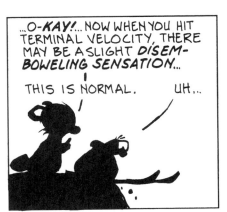

...O-*KAY!*...NOW WHEN YOU HIT TERMINAL VELOCITY, THERE MAY BE A SLIGHT *DISEMBOWELING SENSATION...*

THIS IS NORMAL.

UH...

"...AND THE STOCKINGS WERE HUNG BY THE CHIMNEY WITH CARE, IN HOPES THAT SAINT NICHOLAS SOON WOULD BE THERE..."

ST. NICHOLAS?

YEAH!... SANTA CLAUS... FATHER CHRISTMAS... KRIS KRINGLE...

THE RED CHIMNEY WEASEL... THE SCARLET SLEIGH-BOY...

WE GET THE PICTURE...

THE BURL IVES CLONE IN THE FLYING-TOY TAXI...

FRY LEWIS

ARE YOU QUITE FINISHED?

...OR PERHAPS JERRY GARCIA?

LEMME GET THIS STRAIGHT... THE SHEPHERD DUDES WERE HANGIN' WITH THE SHEEP WHEN AN ANGEL BEAMED DOWN...

WELL...YES.

FRY LEWIS

DID THEY GET IT ON TAPE?

R.J., THERE WAS NO CNN BACK THEN.

SO HOW DO WE KNOW IT HAPPENED?

IT WAS LEAKED TO THE MEDIA.

BY WHOM?

A HIGHLY PLACED SOURCE.

HMM... SO, THE NEWLYWEDS GET TO B-TOWN, BUT IT'S ALL BOOKED UP 'CAUSE OF THE HEADCOUNTERS' CONVENTION?

NO ROOM AT HOJO'S.

...AND THEN THEY CRASH IN A BARN, THE BABE IS BORN... AND HE GOES ON TO SAVE THE WORLD?...

I ADMIT IT SOUNDS A BIT OVER THE TOP.

WHO GREEN-LIGHTED THIS PROJECT?

I THINK IT WAS SOME GUY AT UNIVERSAL,

TALK ABOUT AN EGO!

FRY◦LEWIS

...AND THESE THREE WISE GUYS FOLLOWED A *STAR* TO THE MANGER BABE?...

FRY◦LEWIS

...*ONE STAR?* THAT'S *IT?*

YA KNOW...

...WITH A LITTLE PROMOTION, THIS KID COULD'VE BEEN *BIG!*

BIGGER THAN THE BEATLES?

QUITE POSSIBLY.

29

...SOME ASSEMBLY
REQUIRED...

31

YA KNOW, VERNE, IT'S ENTIRELY POSSIBLE NORENE'S BABY-TO-BE WILL LIVE TO SEE THE TURN OF TWO CENTURIES!...

WOW.

...OH, THE *WONDERS* THAT KID'LL WITNESS!

TRUE TECHNO-MIRACLES!

I, FOR ONE, CAN'T *WAIT* FOR THE INTRAMUSCULAR, NUCLEAR CHEEZ-WIZ EXCRETION IMPLANT...

FRYo LEWIS

...'IGHT *HERE*... UN-ER AH 'ONGUE!

NEXT TO THE SALSA TOOTHPASTE DISPENSER.

THEY'RE *GONE!*

IT'S *ABOUT TIME!*... I WAS GETTING TIRED OF *BEGGING* FOR FOOD!...

VERNE,.. I'VE BEEN THINKING... WITH NORENE *PREGGERS* 'N' ALL...

... HOW CAN THEY AFFORD TO FEED US *AND* THE *BABY?*

FRY o LEWIS

...HOPE THE KID MAKES IT.

WE CAN TOSS HIM A FEW SCRAPS.

FRY.
LEWIS

I JUST WANT TO SAY HOW *EXCITED* I AM TO BE DIRECTING THIS YEAR'S *ICE-TRAVAGANZA*...

THE '97 PAGEANT'S GONNA BE THE *BEST EVER!*

SO YOU *ARE* EXPANDING MY SKATING TRIBUTE TO *"CONDIMENTS I HAVE LOVED"??*

LIKE I SAID, THIS IS GONNA BE THE *BEST* PAGEANT *EVER*...

THE "EL RANCHO CAMELOT CRIER" CALLED ME *"SPECTACULARLY NOT AWFUL"!!!*

OKAY, LET'S RUN THROUGH THE *MANILOW MEDLEY*...

HEY, R.J.!... YOU'VE PUT MY SOLO *BEFORE* THE PAGEANT AND *DURING INTERMISSION*...

..EVERYONE'LL BE ON A *NACHO RUN!!*

VERNE, *VERNE, VERNE!*

...YOURS IS THE MOST *INTEGRAL* ROLE IN THE *ICE-TRAVAGANZA!!*

IT *IS?*

WITHOUT *YOU* DRIVING THE *ZAMBONI*, WHAT WOULD WE *HAVE?*

UH...

...BUMPY ICE?

YOU THE MAN!!!

BUT R.J., I DON'T *WANT* TO DRIVE *THE ZAMBONI* IN THE ICE-TRAVAGANZA!... I WANT TO *SKATE*, PERCHANCE TO *SOAR!!!*...

GROAN...OH, GET IT OVER WITH...

CUE THE THEME FROM "MANNIX"!!...

UH, VERNE...

REALLY WEAK ANKLES.

MY *FAVORITE COMIC* IN THE "EL RANCHO CAMELOT CRIER" IS *GONE!*...

...AFTER *50 YEARS*, "LI'L URCHIN TIMMY" HAS BEEN REPLACED BY SOME STRIP ABOUT A *COW AND A SNAKE* LIVING OUTSIDE A PLANNED RETIREMENT COMMUNITY!

I THOUGHT YOU *HATED* "LI'L URCHIN TIMMY."

I DID...BUT IN A WORLD THAT'S CONSTANTLY CHANGING, ITS *CONSISTENT MEDIOCRITY* WAS ONE THING I KNEW I COULD *COUNT ON*...

...NOW, WHAT AM I GOING TO DO?

FRY & LEWIS

YOU COULD *HATE* THE *NEW* STRIP.

TOO BIG A RISK...WHAT IF IT TURNS OUT TO BE *GOOD?*...THEN WHERE WOULD I BE?

FINDING THE RIGHT SETTING MAKES *ALL* THE DIFFERENCE.

IT'S SO TRUE.

OKAY, GIMME THE LOG LINE OF THIS MOVIE YOU WANT TO WRITE.

"LOG LINE"?

THE ONE-SENTENCE DESCRIPTION OF THE ACTION...

HMM... TWO GUYS.

STUFF HAPPENS.

THE END.

INTERESTING... BUT WHAT'S THE HOOK?

FRY & LEWIS

...IT'S A TALKIE.

EXCELLENT...

...YA KNOW, YOU CAN'T HAVE TOO MANY SPECIAL EFFECTS.

YOUR *FIRST ACT* SHOULD ESTABLISH YOUR *CHARACTERS* AND THE *OBSTACLE* THEY'LL OVERCOME.

"OUR HERO IS STANDING AT A NEWSSTAND... SUDDENLY A VOLCANO FALLS ON HIM."

TERRAPIN PICTURES

HMM... GOOD... BUT YOU MIGHT WANT TO BUILD MORE SLOWLY TO THE VOLCANO...

HE WAS READING THE SPRING DOUBLE ISSUE OF "PODIATRY TODAY."

THE ONE WITH THE QUARTERLY CORN UPDATE?

FRY & LEWIS

... AND THE "MISS BUNION 1997" CENTERFOLD.

ON TO ACT 2!!

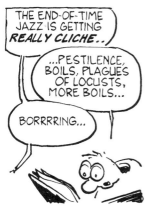

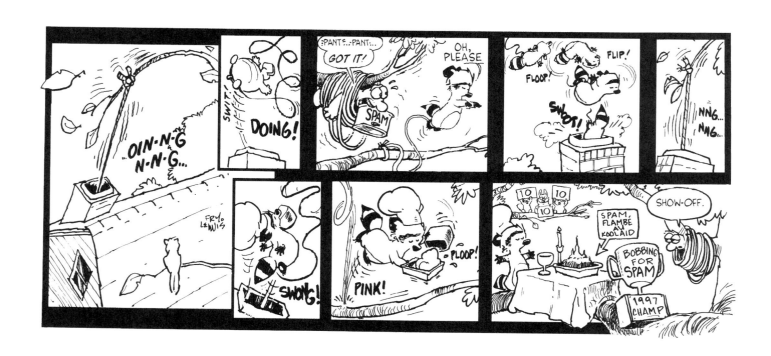

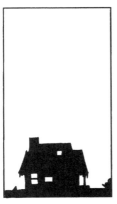

THE PROBLEM WITH *GIRLS* IS THAT THEY GROW UP TO BE...

WOMEN.

WHO INSIST WE EAT WITH *UTENSILS* AND NOT DRY OUR UNDERWEAR IN THE *MICROWAVE.*

MM... TOASTY-COZY

FRY-LEWIS

THEN AGAIN, MAYBE IF WE INTERVENE *EARLY*, WE CAN WIN HER OVER TO THE *DARK SIDE.*

LUKE-ETTE, WE ARE YOUR FATHERS...

OH, HOW *CUTE!*... SHE JUST *URPED* ALL OVER NATE'S SHOULDER.

SEE! SHE'S GOT *POTENTIAL!*

83

86

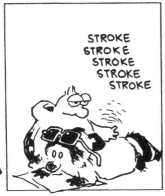
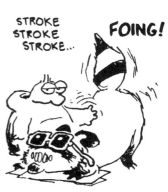

ACCORDING TO OUR EVOLUTIONARY FAMILY TREE, WE'RE *RELATED*!

JUMP FOR JOY.

BUT WHAT DOES THIS *MEAN*?

WE GET TO SPEND HOLIDAYS AND VACATIONS LOCKED IN A SURVIVALIST STRUGGLE AGAINST THE FORCES OF DARKNESS AND QUALITY TIME...

WHAT FUN...

OH WE'RE REQUIRED BY LAW TO HAVE FUN

WOO-HA!

IM AFRAID THAT'S NOT GOING TO CUT IT...

I'M NOT SURE I *WANT* TO BE RELATED TO YOU IF IT MEANS WE HAVE TO *PRETEND* TO HAVE A GOOD TIME!

VERNE... *STRATEGIC PRETENSE* IS THE GLUE THAT KEEPS MOST FAMILIES TOGETHER.

THEN WHAT DO YOU CALL A RELATIONSHIP WHERE YOU DON'T *HAVE* TO *PRETEND*?...

...*FRIENDS?*

FRIENDS.

ALL THIS *REAL EMOTION* IS ENHANCING MY *NATURAL DAMPNESS!*

AGAIN... WITH THE HUGGING.

QUE PASA, O SHELLED ONE?

I THINK MRS. O'MALLEY HAS IT IN FOR MR. O'MALLEY...

...IT'S ONE OF THOSE HUMANE TRAPS.

YOU DON'T SUPPOSE...

...THIS IS ABOUT THAT *3-BEAN SALAD* HE MADE FOR THE NEIGHBORHOOD POTLUCK?

I THOUGHT THE MEXICAN JUMPING BEANS WE SLIPPED IN WERE A GALACTIC IMPROVEMENT.

IT'S THAT TIME OF YEAR...

UH-OH.

"STRRETCH..

OFF WITH THE *OLD*, ON WITH THE *NEW*...

FRYO LEWIS

SHAKE·SHAKE·SHAKE SHIMMY·SHAKE·SHIMMY SHAKE·SHIMMY·SHAKE SHAKE·SHAKE·SHAKE

NEXT YEAR CAN YOU PLEASE SHED DOWNWIND?

I GUESS NOW I'LL HAFTA WASH THESE...

IT NEVER REALLY GETS *QUIET* ANYMORE. THERE'S ALWAYS A RADIO PLAYING, OR A TV...

YEP.

...IT'S AS IF WE'RE ALL *AFRAID* TO BE ALONE WITH OUR OWN *THOUGHTS.*

TOO MANY PESKY QUESTIONS.

FRM. LEWIS

RIGHT!..."AM I *HAPPY?*"... "AM I *SUCCESSFUL?*"... "AM I GETTING ENOUGH *CHEESE?*"

YOU *GOTS* TO DROWN IT OUT!

PAT BOONE: *"IN A METAL MOOD"*?

DITTO.

SMOOOKE ON THE WA-TER...

111

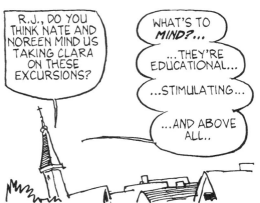

123